UNCOOL

First published in 2007 by
Zest Books, an imprint of Orange Avenue Publishing
35 Stillman Street, Suite 121, San Francisco, CA 94107
www.zestbooks.net

Created and produced by Zest Books, San Francisco, CA
© 2007, 2011 by Orange Avenue Publishing LLC
Illustrations © 2007 by Kristin Bowler

Text set in Mrs. Eaves; title and accent text set in Hot Coffee

Library of Congress Control Number: 2007923349
ISBN-13: 978-0-9772660-7-4
ISBN-10: 0-9772660-7-9

CREDITS
EDITORIAL DIRECTOR: Karen Macklin
CREATIVE DIRECTOR: Hallie Warshaw
EDITOR: Karen Macklin
ILLUSTRATOR: Kristin Bowler
COVER DESIGNER: Tanya Napier
GRAPHIC DESIGNER: Cari McLaughlin
PRODUCTION ARTIST: Cari McLaughlin

PRINTED IN CHINA
LEO 10 9 8 7 6 5 4 3 2
4500271342

*Every effort has been made to ensure that the information presented is accurate. The publisher
disclaims any liability for injuries, losses, untoward results, or any other damages that may result
from the use of the information in this book.*

UNCOOL

A girl's guide to *mis*fitting in

Erin Elisabeth Conley

ZEST BOOKS

SO SOME DAYS YOU FEEL A LITTLE ... UNCOOL.

Maybe you don't rule the school (whatever that means). Maybe you can count your friends on one hand. Maybe the people you do hang out with are more "out" than "in." So?

IT'S COOL TO BE UNCOOL.

All it means is that you don't fit the mold. You don't adhere to the status quo. You're unique, quirky, **INTERESTING**. Different.

Maybe you like to read poetry, make art, or build weird crap that flies. Maybe you're a budding fashion designer or bass player or marine biologist. Maybe you're still figuring out exactly who you are and who you want to be. But you know this: You'd rather be considered a little bit of a misfit than be like all the other clonetards. Still ... there's no denying that *mis*fitting in can sometimes be a **REAL** pain in the neck. Choosing to be authentically you, **QUiRKS** and all, isn't always the prettiest or simplest path. That's where *Uncool* comes in handy.

Here, you'll ponder the social world around you, learn the all-important Rules of Misfitness, and gain a better understanding of your arch nemesis. You'll also get pointers on how to refine your fashion aesthetic and how to handle frenemies. You'll learn to align yourself with fellow **FRee** thinkers and how to figure out where you *mis*fit in.

You'll be guided through the sucky parts of being socially on the **FRiNGe** and find out how great it is to be awesomely, independently, absolutely yourself. Along the way, you might even realize you're more "uncool" than you thought. Which, of course, only makes you that much cooler.

TABLE OF CONTENTS

1. FREAKS, GEEKS, AND ALL THE REST: SORTING OUT YOUR SOCIAL SCENE... 11

The Pecking Order 12

You Are Where You Eat 14

Branded 18

Can't Judge: 20 Books About Insiders,
Outsiders, and Life Forms in Between 20

Peer Pressure Cooker 22

Members Only 24

The School of Cool 26

2. DOWN AND OUT: THE SUCKY SIDE OF MISFITNESS ...29

Sucks to Be 30

With Friends Like You, Who Needs Friends?... 32

Getting (and Spreading) the Juice 34

Which Is Worse? 36

You Gotta Fight: 15 Songs for Underdogs 38

If Only: Fantasy Penalties for
Jocks and Jerks 40

Utterly Uncool Moments 42

Stupid Things Adults Say to Ease the
Pain (Not) 44

Dear Bane-of-My-Existence Letter 48

Friends With the Enemy 52

3. POPULAR, SCHMOPULAR: WHY IT'S COOL TO BE UNCOOL 57

Rules of Misfitness 58

Geek Chic 62

Power Grab: 20 Movies Where the
Little Guy Plays Big 66

New Kid on the Block: 10 Reasons Why
Moving Is Not the End of the World 68

Fabulously Bad Fads 70

Misfit to a Tee 74

No Peaking (Too Early, That Is) 76

4. LET YOUR FREAK FLAG FLY: LIBERATING YOUR INNER MISFIT 79

Salute to the Square Peg 80

Vive la Difference! 82

Trendsetting and Sole-Searching 84

Flock Fitting-In Party 88

Cool Made Simple 92

Taste Test 94

Chinese Fortune Kooky 98

Icons of Cool 106

Pop Quiz! Are You as Open-Minded as
You Think? 108

5. GO BEYOND COOL: INDISPENSABLE MISFIT SURVIVAL TIPS 115

What Matters Most 116

Wouldn't It Be Cool If 118

Music Appreciation: 15 Feel-Good
Freak Songs 120

Love Letters 122

High School High, High School Hell 124

New Mindset Mantras 126

FREAKS, GEEKS, AND ALL THE REST: SORTING OUT YOUR SOCIAL SCENE

THE PECKING ORDER

Have you ever watched monkeys at the zoo groom each other? What about documentary footage of elephants circling round to mourn a dead member of their herd? Or, at the dog park, have you noticed how some pooches seem to naturally rule the pack, while others get picked on? Sometimes it's alarming how little we differ from

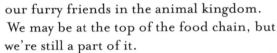

our furry friends in the animal kingdom. We may be at the top of the food chain, but we're still a part of it.

Like most animals, human beings tend to run in packs. And within any pack or in any group setting (think schools, parties, clubs, and teams), there are usually leaders, followers, and a bunch of people in between. Ultimately, there's a sort of hierarchy—or pecking order. When you're near the bottom, this pecking order can be depressing. It sucks to get pecked on! When you're at the top, it can be surprisingly unnerving. After all, there's nowhere to go but down.

But the pecking order is not absolute. It can and will fluctuate over time, and it changes depending on the setting. The most-popular "popular girl" may seem like the queen bee at school, but at home she's just a drone. And the ultra-shy guy from fifth period might be a total Casanova at summer camp. You just never know.

So don't make any assumptions about how good (or bad) somebody else has it. And don't get too attached to your pecking status. Good or bad today, it's sure to change tomorrow.

PSST!
real-life quotes
from real teens

A FRAGILE HIERARCHY

❝Part of being popular is making sure that no one challenges it. If everyone likes you, you've got it made. It's *inside* the crowd that you have to watch it. The lower social rankings can't touch you because you're at the top of the social chain and you have allies. However, your allies can turn on you, and you can be out as quick as you were in.❞—15

YOU ARE WHERE YOU EAT

Unfortunately, no matter where you sit at lunch, the turkey burger will probably still taste like Styrofoam. But before you slide your tray down the line to pay for those soggy fries and lifeless salad, take a moment to register the social landscape around you. Ever notice that people tend to self-segregate—lump themselves into familiar clusters—and sit in the same general spot week after week?

People are creatures of habit. It's weird, isn't it?

But if you step outside of it all for a minute—and look at it like, say, an anthropologist—you'll realize that your environment can provide you with surprising clues about its inhabitants, popular culture, and social norms. These clues can be fascinating, or, at the very least, help you better understand and thus navigate your surroundings. So scarf down that grub, and grab a pencil and a notebook: It's time to conduct a little study on human behavior. First, recruit a trusted cohort to help you make some detailed cafeteria observations. Then, begin drawing up a map of your eating grounds.

On your map, note who colonizes each sector of the cafeteria, dining hall, or courtyard. Include sketches, a key, color-coding, and whatever else you can think of. The more detail you include, the more fun you'll have making it. Remember to include yourself and your friends—like it or not, you're a part of this landscape. And try not to attach simplistic or ordinary stereotypes to anyone—just be straightforward with your descriptions. Don't be petty, and don't create anything you wouldn't share with the rest of the humanoids present.

Once you've made your map, consider the bigger questions, like: How did it get to be this way? What's in flux, and what's always the same? What has changed or is likely to, and why? And, most important, how did *you* end up planted where you are?

Even if you're perfectly content in your spot, are more of a lunch nomad, or just don't give a rat's rear where anybody sits, this exercise might still be illuminating. And who knows? It just might make you think twice before spending the next three years at exactly the same lunch table.

real-life quotes from real teens

NEVER REALLY ALONE

❝As long as I know I've got friends who love me, I'm fine sitting in a corner all by myself.❞ —13

BRANDED

There's nothing wrong with labels — as long as they're stuck on a can (or box or bottle or back pocket of your jeans). But when it comes to labeling *people*, well, that's an entirely different subject.

Sure, we've all felt the slap.

Maybe you've been branded the class kiss-up, the freaky tree hugger, the superficial mall rat, or the wanna-be gangsta. Maybe a girl in a higher grade called you a slut for no apparent reason at all. While some labeling is harmless (like when your mom calls you the "brainy daughter"), most of it is usually misguided and often just plain wrong. And once you've got a label, it tends to stick for seemingly *ever*.

So why do people feel the need to classify others? For some, it's an easy way of trying to make sense of their social universe. For others, it's a lazy way out of really getting to know someone. And, for a few, it's a fugly way to make them feel better about themselves.

18

But you probably already know all this. Deep down, you know that no one is as simple as one or two or even three words. No one is as marginal as what can be written on a name tag.

Even though some say that there is an ounce, a sliver, a microscopic amount of truth to stereotypes (isn't that how they got to be stereotypes in the first place?), people are complex. Most of us are a big jumble of things—constantly changing things—and sometimes the jumble surfaces in confusing ways. The sad clown, the insecure beauty queen, the lonely bully. The world, like its inhabitants, is not clear-cut. It is filled with blurry lines and people who are multidimensional and multifaceted.

Besides, most people continue to evolve. So just because some chick may have been a mall dweller at one point, that doesn't mean she'll be camped out at the food court eternally. Thankfully, this rule goes for you, too. If it didn't, you'd still be sporting the same old jeans you refused to take off in the fifth grade. But you're not. (Are you?)

can't JUDGe: 20 BOOKS ABOUT Insiders, Outsiders, and Life Forms in Between

1. *Will Grayson, Will Grayson* by David Leviathan

2. *The Absolutely True Diary of a Part-Time Indian* by Sherman Alexi

3. *Freak Magnet* by Andrew Ausen

4. *Ghost World* by Daniel Clowes

5. *How to Say Goodbye in Robot* by Natalie Standiford

6. *How to be Popular* by Meg Cabot

7. *The Perks of Being a Wallflower* by Stephen Chbosky

8. *Monster High* by Lisi Harrison

9. *Lizard* by Dennis Covington

10. *Kick Me: Adventures in Adolescence* by Paul Feig

11. *After the Death of Anna Gonzales* by Terri Fields

12. *The Planet of Junior Brown* by Virginia Hamilton

13. *The Scarlet Letter* by
   Nathaniel Hawthorne

14. *The Outsiders* by S.E. Hinton

15. *Geeks* by Jon Katz

16. *Seconds Helpings: A Novel*
   by Megan McCafferty

17. *Define "Normal"* by
   Julie Anne Peters

18. *The Queen Geek Social Club*
   by Laura Preble

19. *Odd Girl Speaks Out: Girls Write
   About Bullies, Cliques, Popularity,
   and Jealousy* by Rachel Simmons

20. *Stargirl* by Jerry Spinelli

Peer Pressure Cooker

You've heard about it, read about it, and been warned (ad nauseum) against its evils ... but peer pressure is definitely out there, and it's intense. It can engulf you in ways so subtle you didn't even know you were feeling the heat. Maybe you get coaxed by the "cool kids" into skipping chemistry class, even though you are really fired up to hit the lab and ignite your Bunsen burner. Or maybe you start wearing itty-bitty thong undies like all of your friends even though you think they feel like a perma-wedgie. The cooker can make you do things you don't want to do—or *not* do things you *do* want to. And most people don't even realize they're being cooked.

Humans are not alone in this follow-the-leader game. A recent study at Emory University in Atlanta, Georgia, found that even chimpanzees feel the need to conform to the behavior of others in their peer group. Like Gwen Stefani says, this sh@# is B-A-N-A-N-A-S.

But before you start isolating yourself or check into the local monastery, keep in mind that peer pressure isn't all bad. It can make you want to get better grades so you can go to a good college, or it can make the class *biatch* act like a nicer person just because she sees her friends doing it.

The important thing to remember is that you have a mind of your own. So use it. And here's a tip: The surer you seem about your ideas and decisions, the less likely anyone is to challenge you.

PSST!

real-life quotes from real teens

UNCOOKED

❝ The cool kids, by my definition, are the ones who stand up for people, themselves, and what they believe in. They have their own opinions and won't get swept away with the crowd. Just because everyone's doing something or likes something doesn't mean that they'll like it or do it, too. ❞ —14

MEMBERS ONLY

Merriam-Webster defines "clique" (pronounced *click*) as "a narrow, exclusive circle or group of persons" that is frequently "held together by common interests, views, or purposes." Not so bad, right? Well, yeah, except maybe for the "narrow, exclusive" part.

Though you may not have yet memorized the definition of "clique," you probably know what it means. You've likely been in a clique and been left out of one. And you've certainly observed them in action at school, on teams, or at jobs. Kids form cliques, teens form cliques, even your parents participate in cliques. The world is like a clique in motion.

The question is: Why? Do people automatically gravitate toward others like themselves from the get-go, or do those who hang out together simply start to become more and more alike over time. And can someone be in a clique and not be snobbish and cliquey? (The optimistic answer for this one has three letters and ends in s.)

When you're on the *inside* looking out, cliques seem like no big deal. But when you're on the *outside* looking in, they can be painful. If you're without a clique (or, worse, stuck in a bad one), it can feel like you hail from an entirely different and wrong planet.

Unfortunately, when this is the case, there's no real quick fix. It takes time to make changes in your social network. But with a little attention and effort, it can happen. You and a friend can even create your own clique with your own rules—people do it all the time. It could be based on something quirky (like a shared fondness for emo or crocheting), or on nothing much at all (like being born on planet Earth). Or you can enjoy *not* being part of a clique, which leaves you lots of space to have all kinds of friends from different groups and social scenes.

The point, anyway, is not to be part of an exclusive group—it's to cultivate good old-fashioned friendships. It might take a while to find people with whom you truly click, but it's definitely worth the wait.

THE SCHOOL OF COOL

What makes people cool at your school? Is it that they play soccer? Play the guitar? Have parents who make more money than everyone else's?

Maybe it depends on whom you ask. You may think team sports are lame, but the jocks don't see it that way. Or you may find drama a big bore, but the thespians undoubtedly feel differently.

If you feel like a misfit, there's a good chance that what's cool at your school is not cool to you.

Take some time to stop and analyze how you and your school's universe jibe (or don't jibe) together by filling out the chart on the following page. It might give you some clues as to why you feel out of the loop—and where you

	COOL at SCHOOL	COOL to YOU
People		
Qualities		
Things		
Hobbies		

COOL TO WHOM?

" To me, it isn't important to be cool. Besides, what other people think is uncool is usually cool after all. " — 13

DOWN AND OUT: THE SUCKY SIDE OF MISFITNESS

SUCKS TO BE ...

Even if you're pretty pleased with who you are and where you fit in, there are bound to be days when it feels like it sucks to be you. (If not, you might be from another planet. Double-check with your parental unit to be sure.)

On those days, it's helpful to have an outlet for your emotions. Physical outlets—like rock climbing, karate, skateboarding, and yoga—are excellent release valves. So is listening to or playing music, and journaling (aka venting on paper) is surprisingly cathartic.

But for days when you're just plain pissed off at the world and don't feel like doing any of the above, have a go at this Mad (at the World) Lib. Write in pencil, or photocopy it before you start, so you can do it more than once. Take no prisoners.

Today, I woke up on the _____ (adjective) side of
the _____ (noun). My _____ (noun) wouldn't
_____ (verb) and my _____ (noun) was all
_____ (adjective ending in 'ed')-up. When _____
(name) looked at me with that _____ (adjective)
stare, I wanted to _____ (verb). Sometimes it really
sucks to be _____ (adverb/noun). Sometimes I just
feel like I'm the only person left in the galaxy that is
not a total _____ (noun). If I could I would
_____ (verb) or wrap up _____ (name) and
have him/her delivered to another _____ (noun).
But then what would I have to _____ (verb) about?
Maybe if I have a _____ (noun) it will help.
Or maybe I should just go to _____ (place)
and _____ (verb).

With Friends Like You, Who Needs Friends?

BFF. It's universal shorthand for what a best friend should be: forever. At least in theory. Unfortunately, in real life, things sometimes work out differently. Friendship, like lots of other things that *seem* all good, can have a not-so-pretty face—sometimes two. And losing a friend can feel very uncool.

Friendship is complicated. Friends can feel jealous or envious or resentful of each other. They can compete for attention, love, status, popularity, power, and reputation. They can argue over who first saw the cool striped hoodie you both covet, or who first saw the new cutie at school who's wearing that cool striped hoodie. Occasionally, these kinds of issues can cause a friendship to end. The "breakup" can be mutual—or not. Sometimes you see it coming. Other times it hits you like a freight train. One day you're best friends, the next you're ex-friends. Even when it's honestly nothing personal—just that you grew apart—getting dumped by a friend is never fun. Of course, when it comes as a shock or was done in a mean-spirited way, like being ganged up on and ousted from your circle, it's much harder to accept.

But don't waste too much time obsessing over what happened. If you *did* do something dumb, face up to it and apologize. If you know you didn't, you can try asking what the deal is. But don't mope or go undercover for too long. Turn your focus to other things and other people. There are new friends out there who won't turn on you. Eventually, your now former friends may try to become friends again. If that happens, you'll have to decide whether to incorporate them back into your life — or not.

Getting
(and Spreading)
the Juice

Gossip is nothing new. Scientists recently unearthed hieroglyphics that prove even the ancient Egyptians liked to dish dirt. People like to talk—always have, always will. And they like to talk about other people. From time to time, you might be that other person.

Unfortunately, you can't tie other people's tongues. But you *can* choose to rise above by not biting back.

It's also important to realize that, even when gossip feels entirely personal (like hearing that friends were going all tabloid about how pathetic it is that you still have a thing for your ex), it's not necessarily so. Sometimes people feel the need to put other people down to make themselves feel better. Of course, no matter the reason, being blabbed about behind your back hurts.

But gossip isn't always all bad. Sometimes we gossip to bond or work out things we don't understand, or even out of concern for our friends. Sometimes it can be fun to gossip with a sister or close friend. Remember, however, that there's a difference between gabbing or analyzing the behavior of mutual acquaintances, and people-bashing or spreading rumors. The trick is recognizing the difference between the good and the gory.

How do you do that? Check your gut. Gory gossip is what you wouldn't say if the gossipee were standing there listening. It's also just generally meaningless and unkind. A good rule of thumb is: If it makes you feel guilty, funny, or uneasy after you engage in it, try to keep your pie hole a little more in check next time.

WHICH IS WORSE?

Losing the school election to your biggest rival *OR*	having all your friends forget your b-day?

Going to prom with your little brother *or*	sitting home alone that night?

Being uninvited to *the* party of the year **OR**	being invited ... to serve hors d'oeuvres?

Freezing up during an oral report *or*	blushing every time you say hello?

Accidentally telling the school gossip your biggest secret **OR**	moving to a new school?

Overhearing your BFF
trash-talking you   **OR**

having your BFF learn
that you were trash-
talking her?

Wearing the same outfit as
the principal on the first
day of school   *or*

accidentally letting one
fly in class?

Getting caught tap-
dancing down the hall by
the most popular person
in school   *OR*

having a massive break-
out on picture day?

Losing all of your friends *or* never having any?

YOU GOTTA FIGHT:
15 SONGS FOR UNDERDOGS

1. "Smile"—Lily Allen

2. "Loser"—Beck

3. "No Rain"—Blind Melon

4. "One Way or Another"—Blondie

5. "Under Pressure"—David Bowie and Queen

6. "Fitting in With the Misfits"—The Eels

7. "There's Always Someone Cooler Than You"
   —Ben Folds

8. "Good Riddance (Time of Your Life)"—Green Day

9. "Here It Goes Again"—OK Go

10. "Stupid Girl"—P!nk

11. "Creep"—Radiohead

12. "Spectacular Views"—Rilo Kiley

13. "Dummy"—Emma Roberts

14. "Chia-like, I Shall Grow"—Say Anything

15. "Emperor's New Clothes"—Sinead O'Connor

IF OnLY: FanTaSY PenaLTieS FOR JOCKS anD JeRKS

THE CRIME	THE PENALTY
The Bully	Compelled to punch himself/herself in the face every hour, on the hour.
The Excluder	Birthday forgotten by friends and entire family for next 10 years.
The Snob	Forced to wear moth-eaten hand-me-downs one size too small.

The Gossip . . . . Sentenced to spend six months in a soundproof glass box in the middle of the cafeteria.

The Fair-Weather
Friend . . . . Small black rain cloud lands permanently on forehead.

The Mocker . . . . Lips mysteriously sewn together.

The Backstabber . . . . . . Forced to sleep on bed of pins and needles.

The All-Around Idiot . .

UTTERLY UNCOOL MOMENTS

Here's what some real-life girls had to say about their most mortifying moments.

PSST!
real-life quotes
from real teens

BOTTOMS UP

❝I was at camp, and I had just begun to make friends with the older kids. I was having the best time, especially when I hung around with this guy I REALLY liked. One day, I saw all of them down on the camp's dock, and I ran down the swim path. I said, 'Hey!' and they all looked up. Suddenly, I tripped and went flying into the water. I looked at them, and they were all laughing. All of a sudden, the bottom of my swimsuit floated to the top of the water. My crush almost died laughing. That's when I knew I wasn't cool and decided to hang with people my own age.❞—15

BONE-A-FIDE DISASTER

❝Oh, man. So, I broke my arm. It was unpleasant. I got back to school after said incident, arm most thoroughly casted, and I noticed that a kid I kind of knew had similar skeletal issues. I decided I'd comment. Trying to decide whether to say, 'How'd you break your bone?' or 'Feeling any better?' I ran into him and burst out, 'How's your boner!?'❞—15

PSST!
real-life quotes from real teens

WRONG FOOT FORWARD

❝Well, there was this guy who was a year older than me. He was in a few of my classes, and I enjoyed talking to him. One day, I stopped to talk to him in the hall. I tried to act really coy and calm, but inside I was screaming. He made a comment about an answer I had missed during class. I gave him a hurt look and flipped my hair. Then, swiveling my hips to look really smooth, I walked away … and fell off of my heel and flat on my face!❞—15

STUPID THINGS ADULTS SAY TO EASE THE PAIN (NOT)

Maybe it's some magical chemical change that happens as you get older, or simply that too many years have lapsed since youth, but lots of times parents just don't get it—at all. They just can't stand it when their offspring hit a rough patch. Undoubtedly, it's because they love you, and they know it's painful and scary. And, possibly, somewhere deep down, they're afraid it's their fault. (Wouldn't it be nice if we really *could* blame them for everything?) They just want it to be better for you. And yet there's not much they can do about it.

Of course, sometimes their life experience (aka wisdom) can really help put what's fuzzy into perspective. And since you can always choose to ignore advice, asking for it is almost always worth a try.

On the other hand, sometimes (lots of times), your 'rents just give *bad* advice. Any of these less-than-inspiring nuggets sound familiar?

- But this is the best time of your life!

- I'm sure s/he didn't mean it.

- Things aren't really that bad. They just *feel* bad.

- Relax.

- It's best to keep busy. Why don't you get up and go mow the lawn or empty the dishwasher?

- Well. *I* think you're cool. And so does Grandma.

- When I was young ... (blah, blah, blah).

- Difficulty builds character.

- You're better than them anyway.

- It's what's inside that counts.

By now, your parents are probably somewhat predictable when it comes to giving advice. And you've probably vowed at least once never to react the way they did to a certain situation when (or if) *you* have kids. For fun, grab some paper and a friend (or, even better, a sibling) and see if you can each predict what your parents would say about the below scenarios. Then think about how you would advise them to respond. Compare answers and have a good laugh. If you're really brave, you can even try the scenarios out on your parents to test your accuracy.

Scenario 1: You studied hard and knew your stuff, but you suffered a serious brain freeze during your geometry final. You're sure you tanked it, and anything less than a 72 percent means summer school with a bunch of cretins.

What your folks would say: _____

_____

_____

What they should say: _____

_____

_____

Scenario 2: You left the peroxide on too long while dying your faux hawk and now your hair is coming out in sad little clumps.

What your folks would say: _____

_____

_____

What they should say: _____

_____

_____

Scenario 3: There's a (false) rumor going around school that you've been making out with every member of the soccer team. Your best friend has been spreading it.

What your folks would say: _____

_____

_____

What they should say: _____

_____

_____

DEAR BANE-OF-MY-EXISTENCE LETTER

We've all got that special someone who appears to have been born just to torment us. Maybe it's a neighborhood thug, class bully, former friend, or all-around arch nemesis. Maybe you've tried to make peace or simply wished them away. But there she is, still staring you down with the stink eye and hassling you in the hall.

What to do? How about write your very own get-a-life letter? Even if you don't send it (probably better not to), it'll feel good to get it down on paper.

See the list on the following pages to fill in the blanks.

Dear _____ ,
use code name for privacy

I don't know if you know this, but I think you're a real

_____ . I've tried to figure out why you're
choose from list A

_____ , but nothing seems to make sense.
choose from list B

Apparently, I'm not alone. Even your _____
choose from list C

thinks you should _____ . I know you're
choose from list D

probably just _____ , but I still believe you'll
choose from list E

end up_____ . If you weren't so_____ ,
choose from list F   *choose from list G*

I'd try to forgive you. Oh well. Now, buzz off and

_____ !
choose from list H

Good luck in life cause you're going to need it,

_____
Fill in your name here

A

tool
waste of breath
poser

B

so obsessed with me
on the planet
such a total imbecile

C

granny
mother
entire family

D

be locked up
seek therapy
have a lobotomy

E

jealous
too stupid to know better
plain old mean

F

kissing my rear
licking my boots
begging to be my friend

G

hideous
rotten to the core
useless

H

bother somebody else
die young
move to another state soon

FRIENDS WITH THE ENEMY

We all try hard to avoid our enemies. But some philosophers say it's not the way to go.

Sun Tzu, the sixth-century Chinese thinker and author of *The Art of War*, famously suggested keeping "your friends close and your enemies closer." That might seem like a majorly misguided idea at first. But before you write off his advice, take a moment to really think about it.

What exactly is this Tzu guy suggesting? That you're supposed to try to be friends with someone cruel, nasty, or unkind? That you should take that incarnation of evil from sixth period (aka girl who steals your boyfriends and ideas) out to coffee? No. But he probably does mean that you shouldn't just ignore her entirely (which is not to say you should confront or antagonize her directly either).

Basically, the idea is that with your enemies close, you have a better chance of knowing what they're up to—what motivates them, and why they think and act like they do. Once you understand them, you can find better ways of handling them. There's even a slight chance that, if you get to know them, you might—God forbid—like them.

It's easy to dismiss your arch nemesis as pure alien evil, but, if you really think about it, you probably have more in common than you'd like to admit. Even if you don't end up being friends (and she continues to act like a jerk), it's nice to try to empathize and better understand who you're up against. Suck it up, open your heart, and fill out the chart on the next pages—even if it initially makes you want to puke. Once you're finished you can feel justifiably superior, knowing that you took the high road rather than the low one.

ARCH NEMESIS (use code name for privacy):

_____

QUALITIES HIS/HER MOTHER MIGHT LIKE ABOUT HIM/HER

NICE GESTURES WITNESSED

THINGS YOU HAVE IN COMMON
(HOBBIES, FRIENDS, THINGS)

....

....

....

....

....

SPECIAL TALENTS OR SKILLS

....

....

....

....

....

....

POPULAR, SCHMOPULAR: WHY IT'S COOL TO BE UNCOOL

RULES OF MISFITNESS

Of course, it goes without saying that the only real hard and fast rule of misfitness is that there are no real hard and fast rules of misfitness.

In other words, as a misfit you're free to chuck what you like. You can toss this entire list and make up your own. Or just weed through it, adding and editing as you please. You can choose to love it, skip it, like it, or lump it. You can pray to it, curse it, or condemn it to eternal damnation. You can chew it up and spit it out when no one (or someone) is looking. And if you're feeling really feisty, you can tear out the page with your bare hands, then make tiny paper shoes with it for your bare fingers. Or, even better, make a little paper boat and launch it in the gutter. Set it—and yourself—free! Or just read it. That's a form of freedom, too.

The Unrules:

★ Be kind to your fellow misfits.

★ Believe that black is a color suitable for any occasion, worthy even of being added to the rainbow.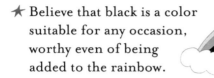

★ Think. Be. Think and be different.

★ Throw caution to the wind. Take chances with fashion, hobbies, hopes, and dreams.

★ Be OK with wearing things that your mother, grandmother, or nosy old neighbor thinks are ugly.

★ Don't be afraid to look weird.

★ Write a blog. Make a documentary film. Publish a zine. Learn the accordion. Build a radio-controlled blimp.

★ Express your individuality in a healthy, creative way.

★ Let your inner geek speak—whether it's through music, art, science, origami, circus school, or whatever.

★ Do something slightly risky (but never dangerous) every once in a while. Take up the sport of spelunking (cave exploring), or invite your gym teacher to join you for lunch.

★ Have patience with people who are different from you. (You know, the ones who are so "normal" they're practically clones.)

★ Find something to believe in, a worthy cause of sorts. Volunteer and invest some genuine spirit into it.

★ Feel free to pop over to the Dark Side, but don't move there.

★ Orbit Planet Normal in your mother ship, but don't inhabit it.

★ Don't change just because someone else thinks you should.

★ Know that even though you may misfit, there's always someplace you are welcome in the world.

PSST!
real-life quotes
from real teens

COOL WITH BEING UNCOOL

❝I'm kind of an outcast anyway. People think I'm kind of weird because I'm different than everyone else. But I don't think it's that important to be cool.❞—13

Geek Chic

Historically, hyper-studious types have drawn the short stick in terms of pop culture portrayals. They tend to be depicted in a bumbling, pathetic light as sporting thick, taped-together black-framed glasses—and having little luck with the opposite sex. They're seen as nerdy antifashion types, clad in suspenders and orthopedic shoes, who never get out of the house, are best friends with their chemistry kits, and would probably make out with a textbook if they could.

In reality, "geeks" are often some of the most fascinating people on the planet. They may stumble a bit socially, but they also have some incredibly sweet skills. Check out the list of six below to get a small sample of just how hot (and cool) brainy can be.

Tatiana Cooley (1972–)

Multiple-time USA National Memory Champion. Given just 15 minutes to memorize 100 faces and names, she'll spit back 70 of them, no problem. Can also remember random strings of numbers or words and lines of poetry like magic. Notoriously absentminded, would probably implode without Post-its. Reads books in Portuguese, Spanish, and English.

Albert Einstein (1879–1955)

German-born Nobel Prize-winning scientist and serious genius. Discovered the theory of relativity ($E = mc^2$). Pacifist and progressive thinker. In 1999, *Time* magazine named him Person of the Century. Had crazy hair, sported rumpled fuzzy sweaters. Light-years ahead of his time.

Bill Gates (1955–   )

Computer nerd and cofounder of Microsoft. Is currently one of the wealthiest dudes in the world. *Time* named him (along with his wife and U2's Bono) the 2005 Person of the Year for his humanitarian efforts. Has little round glasses and geeky hairdo, and favors pleated pants.

Mahatma Gandhi (1869–1948)

Celebrated Indian spiritual leader and nonviolent freedom fighter. Fought for social change in India and against racism in South Africa. His name, Mahatma, means "great soul." Skinny, bald, and had a flair for funny shoes. Inspired the likes of Martin Luther King Jr.

Danica McKellar (1975–   )

Actress and math whiz who graduated with highest honors from UCLA. Played the beautifully awkward Winnie Cooper on the critically acclaimed late '80s–early '90s TV series *The Wonder Years* and proved her own mathematics theorem offscreen. Was a featured speaker at Stanford University's 2006 conference Proof and Prejudice: Women in Mathematics. Had to suffer through puberty on national TV. Came out the other side a major babe and geek magnet.

SpongeBob SquarePants (1999–)

Charming, cheerful, and optimistic sea sponge with a huge international legion of fans. Masterful fry cook who excels at number-driven activities. Can sing and play the guitar and ukulele. Cursed with buckteeth and perma-goofy grin. Wears tighty whities, kneesocks, and dorky short pants. Possesses the ability to morph into other shapes and regenerate own limbs.

PSST!
real-life quotes
from real teens

COOL DEFINITION

❝I define cool as someone who is original—someone who stands up for people younger or weaker than themselves.❞ —15

POWER GRAB:
20 MOVIES WHERE THE LITTLE GUY PLAYS BIG

1. *Scott Pilgrim vs. the World* (2010)

2. *It's Kind of a Funny Story* (2010)

3. *Bandslam* (2009)

4. *Happy Feet* (2006)

5. *Dodgeball: A True Underdog Story* (2004)

6. *Mean Girls* (2004)

7. *Napoleon Dynamite* (2004)

8. *Sleepover* (2004)

9. *Real Women Have Curves* (2002)

10. *Spellbound* (2002)

11. *New Best Friend* (2002)

12. *O* (2001)

13. *She's All That* (1999)

14. *Romy & Michele's High School Reunion* (1997)

15. *Bottle Rocket* (1996)

16. *Welcome to the Dollhouse* (1995)

17. *Edward Scissorhands* (1990)

18. *Heathers* (1989)

19. *Hairspray* (1988)

20. *The Breakfast Club* (1985)

New Kid on the Block: 10 Reasons Why Moving is Not the End of the World

Kermit the Frog once lamented that "it ain't easy being green." Truer words were never spoken by a frog puppet with a hand stuffed up his rump. It's tough being the newbie, but it isn't the end of the world. In time, some other sucker will move in and relieve you of this dreadful title. Until that's the case, consider the following reasons *not* to lose your cool if you're forced to suffer through a move.

1. There will be a big going away party thrown in your honor.

2. Your friends from your old hood will shoot tons of sweet "We miss you!" emails, IMs, texts, and calls your way.

3. Out of guilt, your parents or guardians will heap lots of sympathy (and bribes) upon you.

4. You'll be forced out of the same-old same-old, which is almost always a good thing, even if a little painful at first.

5. It's a chance to expand your social network and up your friend count.

6. It's a new opportunity for Cupid's arrow to strike. (In other words, lots of new, unknown cuties!)

7. No more [*insert least favorite teacher, arch nemesis, or neighborhood pest here*].

8. It's a chance to totally reinvent yourself or stay exactly the same — whichever suits your fancy.

9. Tons of new favorite hangouts will be awaiting discovery. Some might even be cooler than the old ones.

10. An object (that's you) in motion tends to stay in motion.

FaBULOUSLY BaD FaDS

Obviously, what's cool is almost impossible to define in specific, concrete terms. Fads and fashions come and go almost as regularly as Earth spins around the sun, and almost as unpredictably as pop quizzes are given.

Forget Loch Ness or Stonehenge. When it comes to the great, unsolved mysteries of all time, current *trends* beat nearly everything on the list.

Consider these fun, funny, and fabulously bad fads that once swept the nation. And remember that if anyone ever hates on your funky fashions or quirky ideas, what they mock today just might make you a millionaire tomorrow.

Cabbage Patch Kids

These pudgy-headed, stumpy-limbed, overpriced dolls look more like little old men than cuddly babies. No two are exactly alike, and in the early '80s kids loved 'em like they were their own offspring. If you didn't get one, it was either the end of the world, or like your parents loved you a lot less than they should have.

Shrinky Dinks

These big floppy bits of plastic that you color and then cook hit the market in 1973. They magically shrink down to little stiff bits of plastic in your very own kitchen oven. Who knew baking plastic could be such fun?

Sea Monkeys

The goofiest and weirdest pet around. These mysteriously multiplying creatures are actually just brine shrimp eggs that hatch in water with a little specially prepackaged TLC. They were really hot in the '60s and '70s.

Chia Pets

The goofiest and weirdest plant around. They come in collectible ceramic shapes (rams, turtles, pigs, puppies, and kittens) that grow a leafy covering when spread with special Chia seed mix and watered. People went crazy for them in the early '80s, and could be heard singing the Chia Pet commercial theme song on the bus.

Pet Rocks

In 1973, these plain old river rocks (aka perfect pets and faithful companions) hit the stores packaged in nifty boxes, complete with birth certificates and owner manuals. The creator made a fortune on them. Can you believe people actually broke open their piggy banks to buy millions of these things?

Troll Dolls

Born in the '60s—a decade that gave birth to some truly kooky crazes—these little guys have funny faces, squatty bodies, and crazy neon hair that melts more than burns when put in a candle's flame. They are still around and still so fugly, they are almost cute. (Almost.)

Leg Warmers

Before these footless kneesocks were the must-have accessory, they were just functional fashion created to keep a dancer's drumsticks toasty. But in the early '80s, they shot to popularity after being featured in movies like *Fame* and *Flashdance*. They came back briefly in 2004. Very briefly.

PSST!

real-life quotes from real teens

COOL TRENDSETTING

❝One time, it was 'twin day' at my school. I was twins with my friend, and we each wore green shirts with cherries, black capris, blue striped socks, black clogs, sparkly blue jackets, and pigtails. Everyone LOVED our outfits.❞ —13

MiSFit to a Tee

Slogan tees are a fun way to express your individuality and quirky perspective on the world. There are tons of funky, telling, and thought-provoking slogans already out there, but you can also write your own and have it printed. See those listed below for inspiration.

YOU'RE BORING

NORMAL ON THE INSIDE

IF YOU CANNOT CONVINCE THEM, CONFUSE THEM

PLEASE, HAVE A NICE DAY ... SOMEWHERE ELSE

No Peaking (Too Early, That Is)

You know those people who seem to have it all: perfect hair, perfect teeth, perfect smile, perfect body, perfect existence? The ones that possess some sort of powerful gravitational pull—that seem to have been plucked from above and placed in the middle of the school universe? The ones that seem to be living proof that life isn't fair? At all?

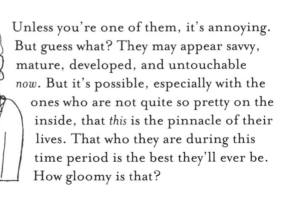

Unless you're one of them, it's annoying. But guess what? They may appear savvy, mature, developed, and untouchable *now*. But it's possible, especially with the ones who are not quite so pretty on the inside, that *this* is the pinnacle of their lives. That who they are during this time period is the best they'll ever be. How gloomy is that?

It's also possible that those who haven't been pre-stuffed with seemingly perfect pixie dust have just not come into their own quite yet.

High school is really just the beginning of your growth period, not the end. Some people hit their stride in college, and some even later in life. If you don't feel like you've entered, or even had a glimpse of, your prime yet, don't fret—it just gives you something to look forward to.

LET YOUR FREAK FLAG FLY: LIBERATING YOUR INNER MISFIT

Salute to the Square Peg

After the 1999 school shootings in Columbine, any and almost all kids on the fringe were looked at in a new, scary, and, for the most part, unjust light. Students who had long hair, wore black, and listened to punk or metal, were seen as potential threats to public safety. It was a sad time, for the family and friends of the victims, for the country, and for innocent outsider types.

Schools are like microcosms of the world. Each has its own unwritten social rules, expectations, and norms— all of which stem from popular culture as a whole. But all you have to do is pick up a magazine or cruise the Internet to know that pop culture is pretty twisted in terms of what it values as important. So you aren't a cheerleader or among the in-crowd—that doesn't mean you're depressed or dangerous. It could just mean that you're not exactly what a lot of TV shows and movies suggest you should be. That's a good thing. Imagine what a snooze life would be if people were all the same.

You probably already know this and may even like being considered an "outsider." But even if you do, it's still good to know that you *do* fit in somewhere, whether it's on your block, on the Ping-Pong team, in the ceramics room, in the science lab, playing music, writing poetry, or hanging out with your best friend. If you're ever feeling like a square peg, remember where you belong, and know there's a square hole in your life somewhere that you can lock into.

FREAK OUT

❝ They call us freaks that do everything unusual and unexpected. But really, we're living, and they're not. ❞ — 13

Vive La Difference!

If you haven't already, you will someday find your tribe, your peeps, your group of *frelatives*. And, based on the ol' "birds of a feather" theory, the people you gel with will be (or already are) a lot like you. It's cool when friends share likes, dislikes, and interests, but if there were no points of difference, you'd never be forced to see or think about things in a fresh way. Eventually, you'd put one another to sleep.

No matter how much you admire someone else, you should have your own style and flair. It would suck to always agree on everything. Commonalities aside, you and your friends are more distinct than you realize.

Want proof? Try going with a few friends to an art gallery to look at an abstract painting or sculpture, or head outdoors, lie down on the grass, and stare up at the clouds. Take a few moments to stare and think before asking one another what you see. Be honest and open. Ask each other what you remember most about a certain event, occasion, or conversation. No doubt there will be some similarities, but there will be lots of variations, too. The same thing sometimes looks totally different through somebody else's eyes.

83

TRENDSETTING AND SOLE-SEARCHING

How you dress is one of the easiest and most fun ways to express your individuality. Of course, it's safer to take your fashion cues from the crowd and shop at the chain store in the local mall. But if you want to cultivate your *own* sense of style and stand out, you have to take some risks. Why wear what's basically a uniform when you don't have to?

Fashion is an art—and the ultimate form of self-expression. But creating your own style doesn't happen overnight. It takes time and research. Start by leafing through your favorite fashion mags to get an idea of what's in at the moment (but not to copy them). You can also head out into the city to people watch, or check out movies from different decades. Aspiring designers also study other designers. Maybe you'll learn that you're all about the funky femme styles of Marc Jacobs, or that you're cuckoo for the crazy-beautiful

creations of Vivienne Westwood. It's always helpful to have a muse to guide you, but once you've got your muse, try to fly free. In the end, the most important thing is to e-x-p-e-r-i-m-e-n-t. It's better to commit the occasional fashion offense, than to be a clone. (Now, *that* would be a crime.)

Tips to Help Set Your Inner Fashionista Free:

- Pay attention to offbeat celebrities, hipsters, and style icons—those who are willing to wear their personalities on their proverbial sleeves.

- Shop at vintage stores and smaller boutiques. Hit garage sales and riffle through your grand-parents' closets.

- Go global and steal style from people from other cultures—like Spanish flamenco dancers, Japanese harajuku girls, and British punks.

◯ Sign up for knitting or sewing classes in your local community. (Bet you didn't know that before 1850, more than 70 percent of all clothes were hand-stitched at home.)

◯ Hit the streets with your digicam. Take shots of anything—and everything—that inspires you. Could be ABC gum stuck on a tree, a cloud, or graffiti. It might spark something in your creative unconscious later.

◯ If you feel sheepish, start by experimenting with shoes, hats, bags, and other accessories. They're a little less intimidating than actual clothing.

MAKING YOUR MARK

❝ Some people go out and buy things because everyone else owns them. I only buy something if I actually like it. ❞ —15

For fun, try to sketch original designs on the figures below. Don't be afraid to go all out and fashion fast-forward. It's often the weird, awkward, and too offbeat looks that are later embraced as hip, new trends.

FLOCK FITTING-IN PARTY

Can't face another lame dance in the gym, afternoon at the mall, or Friday night football game with all the other sheep in the flock? Take charge of your social destiny and throw a Flock Fitting-In Party. It's bound to be better than the standard alternatives, and it might even be a quirky-good time. Invite as many unlike-minded friends as possible who are willing to celebrate difference to the highest pedigree.

SUGGESTED MENU: EXOTIC MUNCHIES

Hors d'oeuvres: kim chee (Korean), edamame (Japanese), samosas (Indian), baba ganoush and pita bread (Middle Eastern)

Starters: green papaya salad (Thai), borscht (Russian), ceviche (Latin American)

Main dishes: sushi (Japanese), pierogi (Polish), falafel sandwiches (Middle Eastern), paella (Spanish), sautéed bok choy (Chinese)

Desserts: baklava (Greek), gelato (Italian), Madeleines (French)

Drinks: Thai iced-tea, Italian soda, café con leche, fizzy water with fresh kiwi or cucumber

SUGGESTED ATTIRE: MISFIT TO THE MAX

- 👕 hand-sewn plaid mini with kneesocks

- 👕 anything made before 1985

- 👕 Japanese kimono

- 👕 vintage tux (with deep-purple ruffled top)

- 👕 lounge singer chic

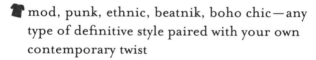

- 👕 personalized Misfit to a Tee T-shirt

- 👕 black

- 👕 mod, punk, ethnic, beatnik, boho chic—any type of definitive style paired with your own contemporary twist

- 👕 whatever you want!

SUGGESTED DECORATIONS: CULT CLASSIC

(Locale: underground-art gallery, warehouse space, urban loft aka friend's garage)

× original art

× posters of antiheroes, cool icons, rebels

× streaming video of anime, classic cult flicks
   (*Rebel Without a Cause*, *Eraserhead*, *Brazil*),
   arty video blogs

NO balloons, paper party hats, or streamers

SUGGESTED ACTIVITIES: SWEET SKILLS

Have a staring (indifferently) contest.

Offer tango or flamenco lessons.

Conduct a poetry slam.

Play too-cool-for-school poker. Bet recklessly with broken tiaras, wallet-sized school photos, or old Barbie limbs.

Make a diorama of the school cafeteria. (Now you can sit wherever you want!)

Swap mortifying misfit moments.

Break-dance, celebrate individuality, and thank the idiosyncratic gods you're you.

COOL MADE SIMPLE

Dying to break from the crowd and dazzle with difference? No matter your budget or your location (small town, big city, something in between), there are simple, not-too-drastic ways to express your individuality—without giving your family a full-blown panic attack.

- Wear vintage.

- Speak your mind.

- When you think something nice about someone, say it.

- If short shorts are in, wear long ones. If everybody's sporting polka dots, try stripes.

- Pursue your passion.

- Take a T-shirt-tearing class and personalize your look.

- Paint your nails an outrageous color.

- Buy a funky wig.

- Get temporary dye and color your hair cotton-candy pink or fishtail blue.

- Learn an instrument, or try out for the school play.

- Create and publish your own zine or graphic novel.

- Befriend an elderly person.

- Decorate your notebooks with cool anime drawings, photo collages, or exotic candy wrappers.

- Do something so unexpected you surprise yourself.

- Be unabashed. Be you.

PSST!
real-life quotes from real teens

COOL RULE OF THUMB

❝What's cool? When you are yourself and don't care about anything else.❞ —13

Taste Test

Butthead (of *Beavis and Butthead* fame) spoke for all of us when he said, "I like stuff that's cool. I don't like stuff that sucks." But, of course, even Butthead knows that what's "cool" is totally personal.

It might feel like someone else is dictating the ITs—the "in" clothes, things, and people—but you have more power than you think when it comes to deciding what's hot and what's not. The truth is, real coolness is *not* letting someone else dictate what's cool—it's figuring it out for yourself.

When it comes to what we like, we usually have pretty strong—and differing—opinions. Sometimes, comically so. Fill in this little grid with your friends to see who is into what. And no laughing at one another's picks … at least not until you're out of earshot.

	COOL	UNCOOL
Soul patches		
I ♡ Mom tattoos		
Skinny jeans		
Black nail polish		
Eyeliner on guys		
Sk8er girls		
Striped leg warmers		
Manga		
Kitten heels		
Short shorts		
Volunteering		
Organized religion		
Unorganized religion		

continued on page 96 ...

	COOL	UNCOOL
Piercings		
Doggie fashions		
Oversized sunglasses		
Bitterness		
Nerdcore hip-hop and geeksta rap		
Sack lunches		
Loving your parents		
Defying your parents		
Celebrity idolization		
Playing chess		
Hello Kitty & Co.		
Converse high-tops		
Following the crowd		
Tighty whities		

	COOL	UNCOOL
Tube tops		
Muscle tees		
Unicycles		
Bling		
Cheerleading		
Tap dancing		
Plaid miniskirts		
Acting like you don't care		
Acting like you do		

PSST! real-life quotes from real teens

CHINESE FORTUNE KOOKY

The Chinese have their own fortune-telling system—
kind of like astrological horoscopes, only different.
Their zodiac is a cycle of animal signs, based on the year
you were born. Each year is represented by one of 12
different animals. Your animal reveals a lot about your
instincts, personality, and general reaction to the world.

Check out the next few pages to find your beast, learn
more about your social nature, and see what the Chinese
charts have to say about you.

YEAR: 1924, 1936, 1948, 1960, 1972, 1984, 1996, 2008 ...

SIGN: **Rat**

In China, rats are seen as a symbol of luck and wealth rather than a sewer dweller. You tend to be a charming leader type and are loaded with ambition. You're likely to run for office or work extra hard in school. You are a loyal friend but tend to hold a grudge. Be careful not to disrespect others when their opinions differ from yours. You click best with Monkeys, Oxen, and Dragons.

YEAR: 1925, 1937, 1949, 1961, 1973, 1985, 1997, 2009 ...

SIGN: **Ox (or Buffalo)**

Strong like a bull, indeed. You are a headstrong and reliable person who can sometimes be on the introverted side, but takes great comfort in close friendships. You are articulate when push comes to shove, but probably not a member of the debate team. Friends might tell you to lighten up from time to time because you tend to take things too seriously. You hit it off well with Snakes and Roosters.

YEAR: 1926, 1938, 1950, 1962, 1974, 1986, 1998 ...
SIGN: **Tiger**
Easy, Tiger! You may not be king of the jungle, but you are definitely the leader of the pack. Others have a tough time resisting your charm and animal magnetism. Your tendency to pounce and be slightly self-centered can sometimes get you into trouble, but you also have a sweet side. Horses and Dogs make good best buds.

YEAR: 1927, 1939, 1951, 1963, 1975, 1987, 1999 ...
SIGN: **Rabbit**
Silly Rabbit. You tend to give people the warm fuzzies and have a wide circle of friends that adore you. You can sometimes be too sensitive and lean on your support network rather than stand on your own two lucky feet. You'd almost rather be pushed around than be forced to fight. Goats and Pigs are a good social match for you.

YEAR: 1916, 1928, 1940, 1952, 1964, 1976, 1988, 2000 …

SIGN: **Dragon**

You might not suffer dragon breath, but you *can* sometimes have a big mouth. People love to listen to you
anyway, because you are smart, talented, and dynamic.
You are a natural leader who doesn't like to cave in to
others. Watch your fiery temper when crossed. You're
best in the company of Monkeys and Rats.

YEAR: 1917, 1929, 1941, 1953, 1965, 1977, 1989, 2001 …

SIGN: **Snake**

People tend to trussssssst in you and are seduced by
your charms. You can be very generous with friends—
in spirit more than with money. You are
disarmingly clever but sometimes
doubt your self-worth. See yourself
as your friends do, and your confidence
is sure to ssssssskyrocket. Roosters and
Oxen are your pals.

YEAR: 1918, 1930, 1942, 1954, 1966, 1978, 1990, 2002 ...

SIGN: **Horse**

You are smart, friendly, and quite independent. Sometimes too independent. You know how to work a room and are rarely left off the guest list. You don't need approval from others to feel sure-footed, and aren't swayed by peer pressure. You like to travel and hate to be penned in. You typically get on great with Dogs and Tigers.

YEAR: 1919, 1931, 1943, 1955, 1967, 1979, 1991, 2003 ...

SIGN: **Ram (or Goat)**

Nothing would make you happier than hanging out in your very own field of dreams. You have a genuine artistic soul and pure imagination. You've been known to put your foot in your mouth but aren't likely to butt heads over it. Take care to keep your anxiety in check, both socially and personally. You can be delightful company when you want to be! Pigs and Rabbits make good friends for you.

YEAR: 1920, 1932, 1944, 1956, 1968, 1980, 1992, 2004 ...
SIGN: **Monkey**
Cheeky Monkey! You're creative, witty, and clever— sometimes too much for your own good (and that of your friends). You like to hang with a funky bunch and have friends from multiple cliques. You tend to be self-indulgent and self-centered, especially because people go bananas over your spirited ways. You play best with Rats or Dragons.

YEAR: 1921, 1933, 1945, 1957, 1969, 1981, 1993, 2005 ...
SIGN: **Rooster**
It's no surprise that you prefer to take charge and rule the roost. You are good at making snap decisions, like what movie to rent or who gets shotgun. You have no qualms about speaking your mind and strutting your stuff. For these reasons, you sometimes come off as a little bit, well, cocky. Be careful to not intimidate or nag others unnecessarily. You like chillin' with Oxen and Snakes.

YEAR: 1922, 1934, 1946, 1958, 1970, 1982, 1994, 2006 ...

SIGN: **Dog**

You are a good listener, faithful sidekick, and loyal friend. But your tendency to be anxious and distrustful leaves you sometimes feeling like you're in the doghouse. You have a strong sense of justice, and are likely to stick up for underdogs and outcasts. You're most compatible with Tigers and Horses.

YEAR: 1923, 1935, 1947, 1959, 1971, 1983, 1995, 2007 ...

SIGN: **Pig**

You may be an oinker, but you are far from crude in dress, style, and manners. You have a very giving spirit, and others sometimes try to take advantage of your generosity. You'd rather not sling mud or fight dirty, but if pushed to the fence you will. You tend to be quite selective about your mates and are sometimes seen as a snob. You get on famously with Rabbits and Goats.

HOLDING THE REIGNS

❝I name the group I'm in. I completely ignore the existence of other groups and simply interact with people that I can stand or find reasonably interesting or amusing. Popular sovereignty is what it's all about. People are only popular because the masses consent to it. If no one consents to appoint someone as popular, then no one is. I don't recognize anyone as popular at my school. The people outside of my social group are amusing little entities that I poke and prod now and again.❞—16

ICONS OF COOL

Some people just seem to exude cool, but it's tough to put your finger on exactly what makes them so cool. They seem to have a certain something—a style or a sense of humor or just a general attitude—that makes them stand out from the crowd.

So, what's cool to you? It's kind of inspiring to try to pin down who your cool archetype is and what s/he embodies. It says a lot about what's important to you and what qualities you admire and why. Maybe you're drawn to brooders like Johnny Depp, do-gooders like Angelina Jolie, or old-school rule-breakers like Audrey Hepburn and James Dean. Or maybe it's the straight-up honesty of your aunt or the oddball humor of your cute biology teacher. Often, it's even several qualities that make up a whole "cool" package.

COOL

In the space below, make a list of at least five people you admire, and write down specifically what makes them so cool. Consider fictional or cartoon characters, as well as famous people. And since you probably know a few real-life cool cats, make sure they get on the list, too.

1._____

2._____

3._____

4._____

5._____

POP QUIZ!
ARE YOU AS OPEN-MINDED AS YOU THINK?

If you feel fine with the fact that you don't always fit
in with the other sheep in the flock, consider yourself
flucky. Not all offbeats have your confident air. But
being confident can sometimes come with certain side
effects—like arrogance or feelings of superiority. Do
you secretly (or not so secretly) judge others for being
who they are—especially if they aren't so cutting edge
or unique? Do you think even the nice "popular" kids
aren't worthy of your time? Take this quiz to find out
just how open-minded you are about the world of
non-freaks around you.

1. You're working the floor at the record shop when
your cousin's friend comes in asking for the latest
[*insert lamest cheesy pop princess here*] CD
and yammering on about how amazing her music
is. You:

A. secretly slip the poor girl a copy of YOUR favorite new indie band's album instead. She'll thank you for it later.

B. point to the door and tell her to try the mall—you don't sell that crap here.

C. fetch the CD for the kid but recommend some decent ones as well.

D. give the girl what she wants then give it another listen yourself. Maybe it's not so awful after all.

2. You and your neighbor have known each other since the shallow end of the pool seemed deep and are still close to this day. But now she's joined the cheer squad and seems to have started following whatever the trend of the moment is, no matter how lame it is. You:

A. lock her in the bathroom and tell her you won't let her out until she promises to become herself again.

B. vow not to talk to her again (though don't tell her why) until she sees the sad, sad error of her ways and comes crawling back as her former genuine self.

C. write an entry in your blog about how it hurts when friends grow apart, especially when one of them loses her mind and starts cheerleading. Then you send her the link.

D. do nothing. Keep hanging out like you used to. Obviously, she's still the same on the inside.

3. The most popular boy in school asks you out on a date. You really like him but find his ultra-conservative friends and yacht club fashion sense embarrassing. You:

A. accept the date but take him shopping at the coolest vintage store in town first.

B. suggest he set sail with someone a little less out of the ordinary than you.

C. say OK, then tell him you guys have to go solo — somewhere discreet and out of town.

D. tell him to name the time and the place, and you're there.

4. Your BFF suddenly starts to LOVE computer
science. That's all well and good, but her new
verbal obsession with programming, microchips,
and keystrokes makes you want to shut down
and reboot. You:

A. tell her what a snooze she is and suggest she try
something more "creative."

B. send her a crippling virus and then stop hanging out
with her.

C. simply tune her and all her lame hi-tech
talk out by wearing your iPod whenever
you're in the
same room.

D. try to take an
interest in
computers
and share your
interests in
return. Maybe
you'll learn
something from
each other.

ANSWERS:
ARE YOU AS OPEN-MINDED AS YOU THINK?

If you answered mostly As:

You may see yourself as a freethinker, but you have a tough time letting others be. You rationalize your occasional desire to change others by reassuring yourself that you're doing a good deed by helping them to be more interesting. It's fine to give people opinions or suggestions, but not to manipulate them. If you open your mind a little, you might just make some new friends outside of your homogenous circle.

If you answered mostly Bs:

You have a very (very) strong sense of self but, daaaang, you're harsh sometimes! Not everyone is as confident or sure of themselves as you are, and some need more time in life to get to a place where they feel free to be whatever they want to be. Some people need the comfort of a herd. Try to remember this next time you feel like devouring an innocent little lamb.

If you answered mostly Cs:

You don't *really* want to slam others that choose not to challenge the status quo, but sometimes you just can't help yourself. This makes you have a tendency to behave passive-aggressively, which is never pretty to witness. Better to be upfront about your feelings. Just remember to be respectful to people, even if you don't necessarily have respect for their ideas or how they act. If you let yourself relax a little, you can learn a lot from people who think differently than you.

If you answered mostly Ds:

You are a very well-adjusted, thoughtful, and open person. You may be quirky or a nonconformist but you're down with all types of people. You tend to hang out with a rainbow of friends and have a rich, if offbeat, social life. Just be careful not to let your own colorful personality be whitewashed by trying too hard to please others.

GO BEYOND COOL: INDISPENSABLE MISFIT SURVIVAL TIPS

What Matters Most

There's a played-out saying that goes, "Don't sweat the small stuff." It may be true, but it can also make you feel like you're petty or spoiled for being upset that a new friend hasn't returned your latest text message, or that your coach left you sitting on the bench until the second half. That's when you respond with the other played-out saying, "Easier said than done."

Sometimes small stuff hurts big time.

In these moments just let yourself feel whatever you feel, but don't wallow for too long. Try making a list of what matters most (or at least what matters *more* than what hurt you). Be as specific as possible. The first item on your list might be how your best friend stood up for you when a shopkeeper wrongly accused you of shoplifting.

The second might be how much your game has improved since you joined the team. It'll help you put those little immediate wounds into perspective.

Oh, and there doesn't *have* to be a disaster for this to be a helpful and good practice. Whipping up such a list when things are totally fine will just make everything seem even better.

A LITTLE PERSPECTIVE

❝I have been called many names, but it's not the words that hurt, it's who is saying them. If a bully said that he or she hated you it wouldn't hurt, but if a friend or relative did, it would be very hurtful emotionally.❞—15

WOULDN'T IT BE COOL IF ...

- eating truckloads of chocolate made your skin flawless?

- homework wasn't such a freakin' drag?

- adults weren't so uptight?

- haters didn't exist?

- we all *could* just get along?

- shoplifting was legal?

- the pep squad started listening to death metal and getting total body tattoos?

- hopscotch and double dutch were Olympic sports?

- tests were optional?

- your pet could speak ...

- but your most-hated teacher could not?

○ hitting Ctrl+X on your keyboard cut annoying people out of your life?

○ you could go back in time and do one thing differently?

MUSIC APPRECIATION:
15 FEEL-GOOD FREAK SONGS

1. "Born This Way"—Lady Gaga

2. "Change"—Taylor Swift

3. "Extraordinary Machine"—Fiona Apple

4. "It's Oh So Quiet"—Björk

5. "Viva la Vida"—Cold Play

6. "Mr. Blue Sky"—Electric Light Orchestra

7. "Damn It Feel Good to be a Gangster"
   —Geto Boys

8. "Wind It Up"—Gwen Stefani

9. "Here (in Your Arms)"—Hellogoodbye

10. "LDN"—Lily Allen

11. "Daydream Believer"—the Monkees

12. "Hey Ya!"—Outkast

13. "I Don't Feel Like Dancin'"—Scissor Sisters

14. "Have a Nice Day"—Stereophonics

15. "Hey There Fancy Pants"—Ween

Love Letters

When was the last time you officially let
the people in your support network
know how thankful you are for their
friendship? You know who they are.
They're the ones who have never
(or hardly ever) failed you—the ones that
would stay on the phone with you for three hours if
you lost the lead in the school play to your least favorite
person on the planet, or who would explain the Pythag-
orean theorem to you (if they could) for the umpteenth
time so you wouldn't fail your geometry test and be stuck
in summer school. These are the people who genuinely
matter in your life. The ones who won't come and go—
the ones that stick.

We spend so much time sweating the trolls in our lives
that we forget to show gratitude for those we cherish.
It's time to show and share the love! So whip out those
colored calligraphy pens, or your computer mouse and
tablet set, to create a handmade token of your gratitude

and affection. You could write a letter and mail it (the old-fashioned way), make a cool card, draw a comic strip, or create a picture collage of the good times you've had together. Get creative and express yourself. No occasion necessary. Your friends will be touched and flattered. You might even score a tear or two of joy if you really go all out.

LOVE THYSELF

❝I know when people talk behind my back, but I have my friends, and they love me, and I don't need the rest. My ultimate goal in life used to be to please everyone, but my best friend taught me that I can't do that, and so the next best thing is to please myself. It's been working for me.❞ —14

HiGH SCHOOL HiGH, HiGH SCHOOL HeLL

Some people will try to tell you that this is the best time of your life. If that terrifies the crap out of you, don't worry: They're probably wrong. Chances are you don't *officially* have all the typical adult responsibilities — like a mortgage, spouse, full-time job, or whole family to feed. But no doubt you do have your own set of stresses, pressures, and responsibilities. School, social expectations, sports, peer pressure, major personal choices, puberty, friends, family, homework, goals, your future, the opposite sex … the list goes on and on. Your life is no small matter — it's a real-life life, and you have to work at negotiating it well.

That's not to say that this time can't be (or isn't already) great. It's just singular and significant. You are straddling two worlds: childhood and adulthood. You're growing and changing emotionally, physically, and mentally. You're realizing all kinds of new things about yourself and the people around you. That can be exhilarating—and confusing. When you can, try to stop and take it all in on a conscious level. Appreciate this time in your life for what it is: a pain and a pleasure.

Most people only do this in retrospect.

You have so much to look forward to after high school— a whole life! And just think ... whether you go on to college, get a job, or travel the world for awhile, once you graduate you'll never again have to ask for a pass to go to the bathroom.

New Mindset Mantras

A mantra is something you say over and over again to remind yourself of a truth that you've forgotten. It's kind of like a spoken meditation. Get comfy, close your eyes, take some deep breaths, and repeat your chosen mantra. Say it aloud (or in your head) at least 10 times, or more if necessary, and you'll remember just how snug it feels to misfit in. It's best to make up your own, but in case you get stuck, here are a few suggestions to get you thinking:

- Those who know me best, love me best.

- Only fools "fit" in.

- I won't let the jerks get me down.

- My good friends Ben and Jerry would never do this to me.

- Girls who wear glasses have the cutest *sses.

- High school might suck, but college is bound to be better.

ABOUT THE AUTHOR

 **Erin Elisabeth Conley** is a freelance writer and editor who lives in Los Angeles, California. She brings her bratty cat Mouche with her wherever she goes. She recently tripped, broke her foot, and felt very uncool.

She extends special thanks to Karen Macklin, editor extraordinaire and superhero, without whose indispensable contributions and critical eye this book would have been a lot less cool.